SIMPLE STORY OF A SOLDIER

Fire Ant Books

Samuel W. Hankins

Simple Story of a Soldier

SAMUEL W. HANKINS

With a new Introduction by John F. Marszalek

THE UNIVERSITY OF ALABAMA PRESS
Tuscaloosa

Typeface: Perpetua

∞

The paper on which this book is printed meets the minimum require-
ments of American National Standard for Information Science–
Permanence of Paper for Printed Library Materials, ANSI Z39.48-1984.

Library of Congress Cataloging-in-Publication Data

Hankins, Samuel W.
    Simple story of a soldier : life and service in the 2nd Mississippi
infantry / Samuel W. Hankins ; with a new introduction by John F.
Marszalek.
        p. cm.
    Originally published: Nashville, Tenn. : Confederate Veteran, 1912.
    Includes index.
    ISBN 0-8173-5157-4 (pbk. : alk. paper)
    1. Hankins, Samuel W. 2. Confederate States of America. Army. Missis-
sippi Infantry Regiment, 2nd. 3. Soldiers—Mississippi—Biography.
4. Mississippi—History—Civil War, 1861–1865—Personal narratives.
5. United States—History—Civil War, 1861–1865—Personal narratives, Confederate. 6. Mississippi—History—Civil War, 1861–1865—
Regimental histories. 7. United States—History—Civil War, 1861–1865
—Regimental histories. 8. Soldiers—Confederate States of America—
Social conditions. 9. Confederate States of America. Army—Military life.
I. Marszalek, John F., 1939– II. Title.
    E568.52nd .H36 2004
    973.7′62′092—dc22

                                                    2004006299

CONTENTS

PREFACE

To fulfill a promise of long standing made to the boys, I give my experiences as a private soldier boy in the War of the States from the early spring of 1861 to its close.

I do not attempt to explain the causes of the war, as that theme engages the attention of the best historians; but I sincerely believe that no truer men ever espoused any cause. Suffice it to say that our leaders were well selected. As chief executive of our Confederacy Jefferson Davis stands the severest tests. Our generals were brave and true. Our women were good and ever faithful, and they have never been reconstructed. The cause of our failure was not in lack of efficient leaders, but of resources.

My personal experiences, with such incidents as came under my own observation in camp, on the march, and in

prison, are given to pay tribute to the merit of my comrades
and people.

SAMUEL HANKINS.

MERIDIAN, MISS., January, 1912.

INTRODUCTION

John F. Marszalek

At one time, Civil War history was primarily the tale of generals moving regiments, divisions, corps, and armies across battlefields, the conflict appearing as a giant game of chess. Although this is no longer the case, modern Civil War historians are still interested in the clash of armies, but now they investigate the impact of battles on society: the men, women, and children who did not carry a weapon yet were essential parts of the war. They are concerned with how the Civil War conflict impacted a town, county, or region and slaveholders and slaves. And what about the soldiers themselves—the nameless, faceless men who died from disease or were shot, maimed, and killed while implementing the orders of their superiors? In short, modern Civil War historians attempt to analyze all aspects of the conflict, thereby producing new insights.

The study of the common soldier has been a particularly important aspect of this modern approach, referred to as a "new military history." Soldiers' lives and experiences in warfare are crucial to understanding how the tide of war waxed and waned, and why the Civil War lasted so long and became the type of war it was. Soldiers wrote letters home telling about their experiences as the bullets flew in combat or when they tried to find ways to fight boredom in between the battles. They kept diaries, some detailed, others only a few lines a day describing nothing more spectacular than the weather. They wrote to their home newspapers telling about their adventures. After the war, some of them wrote memoirs, recalling what their lives were like in those days when, as Union soldier and later Supreme Court justice Oliver Wendell Holmes Jr. put it: "In our youth, our hearts were touched with fire." The common soldiers' experiences in Civil War units were the formative events in their lives. No matter how long they lived or what they did, their civilian activities could not match the excitement and horror of taking part in combat. This was one of the main reasons so many of them joined veteran organizations and, in that way, tried to maintain a tie to the most significant time in their lives.

In 1905 sixty-year-old Samuel W. Hankins—while living in the Soldiers Home in Gulfport, Mississippi—put onto paper his remembrances of his role as a Confederate soldier in the Civil War. His "Simple Story," as he called it, was serialized in the *United Confederate Veteran*'s magazine, *Confederate Veteran,* and also published as a 1912 pamphlet. What makes

Hankins's tale particularly poignant is the fact that he entered the Confederate army when he was only sixteen years old. When the war came to an end in 1865, he was barely twenty. He experienced combat as a teenager, significantly not the only such youngster in both armies. The Civil War, in general, was fought by men (and a few women) who were the age of today's college students.

Hankins was a native of Guntown, Itawamba County, in northeast Mississippi. When secession came in 1861 and the war followed, he joined a company of volunteers from his hometown. In nearby Corinth, his unit merged with nine others from Tishomingo, Tippah, Itawamba, and Pontotoc counties to form the Second Mississippi Infantry Regiment. This unit left by train for Harper's Ferry, Virginia, where, nearly 800 strong, it joined the Eleventh Mississippi, the First Tennessee, and the Fourth Alabama to form a brigade under Barnard Bee. (Later, before dying at First Bull Run/ Manassas, Bee would give Thomas Jackson his nickname "Stonewall.") The Second Mississippi became part of the Army of Northern Virginia.

Despite the shock of Bull Run/Manassas, Hankins said that "the war began in earnest" only in April 1862, when Union General George B. McClellan launched the Peninsular Campaign against Confederate troops under Joseph E. Johnston. Hankins unfortunately came down with measles and ended up in a Richmond hospital, actually a converted tobacco warehouse. He stayed there less than two weeks, finding the place so awful that he promised himself that if anyone ever tried to send him to a hospital again, "they would have to tie me, and I would squeal like a hog all the way" (22).

He got out of the hospital just in time to participate in the battle of Seven Pines and the rest of the Peninsular Campaign. John M. Stone, who would become the longest-serving governor in Mississippi history and later a president of Mississippi State University, commanded Hankins's Second Mississippi regiment. Along with the Eleventh and Forty-second Mississippi and Fifty-fifth North Carolina, Hankins's unit was in a brigade led by Joseph R. Davis, a nephew of the Confederate president. In November 1862, Hankins's brigade was sent to Goldsboro, North Carolina, to try to thwart a Union raid, and his feet were severely frostbitten in the freezing weather. He suffered complications for the rest of his life. In 1863 as the Army of Northern Virginia under Robert E. Lee moved into Pennsylvania and fought the battle of Gettysburg, Hankins's brigade became part of A. P. Hill's Corps and saw combat in the Railroad Cut where a minié ball broke bones in Hankins's foot and incapacitated him. (Hankins recalls that his company, which went into the three-day battle with forty-six men, came out of it with only two.) When Lee withdrew back to Virginia, Hankins and numerous other soldiers were left behind, and he was captured. He ended up in a prisoner of war camp on David's Island, north of Long Island, New York. Eventually, he was paroled to Petersburg, Virginia, where he was placed into a South Carolina hospital because Mississippi did not have such a facility there. Returning home on furlough, he later joined a cavalry unit that fought at Atlanta on July 28, 1864. He was in Selma, Alabama, when the war came to an end.

The strength of Hankins's text does not rest in his battle accounts, because he only talks briefly about combat, but rather in the stories he recounts that illustrate what it was like to be a soldier. There is only a hint of Lost Cause sentiment in his manuscript; he states in the preface that "no truer men ever espoused any cause" and later when he says that "The Creator never made men equal to the Confederate soldier." (62) Otherwise, this is a straightforward narrative of his experiences, "void of bitterness" (4) as the Confederate Veteran editor wrote in the "Explanatory" to Hankins's story. Both Union and Confederate soldiers, in fact, could relate to this Confederate's words because so many of them had faced similar challenges during the war.

Most soldiers, for example, could sympathize with Hankins's first day in the army, when he clumsily tried to march at the orders of an equally befuddled commander. His tale about the vice of gambling and the men's on-and-off religious conversion from it also rang true for both Billy Yank and Johnny Reb. Hankins demonstrates that serving in a Civil War army was no romantic adventure. It was exciting to ride on top of a railroad car while being transported to some new locale, but even then a narrow tunnel approaching quickly dampened such exuberant feelings. The prevalence of diseases such as measles, smallpox, and frostbite that Hankins discusses, and dysentery which is not discussed, demonstrate how difficult a soldier's existence was even out-side the crash of battle. When the air was filled with minié balls, a non-life-threatening wound like Hankins's foot in-jury still caused pain and agony. Medical care was an un-pleasant experience: the sights, sounds, and smells surround-ing it created intense anxiety and further physical pain.

Hankins discusses, in detail, another normally awful Civil War situation, the experience of being a prisoner of war. Unlike many others who lived miserably in places like An-dersonville and Elmira, he had the good fortune to be sent to a pleasant camp. In fact, he praises the Union medical care he received at David's Island, but he later suffered in a Petersburg Confederate institution.

This short book is full of information on a variety of mat-ters with which the Civil War soldier had to contend. The writing is fast paced, and the descriptions are vivid. Hankins does not discuss every aspect of soldier life, but his book will provide the modern reader with a good insight into that life. This memoir, as the *Confederate Veteran* editor phrased it, "teaches a lesson of army life and the horrors of war." (4)

Having read this brief book, however, the modern Civil War devotee will want to delve more deeply into this topic. Fortunately, there are important books available that pro-vide in-depth information and insight. Bell I. Wiley, many years ago, wrote two books that have become classics: *The Life of Johnny Reb: The Common Soldier of the Confederacy* (1943) and *The Life of Billy Yank: The Common Soldier of the Union* (1952). Later, James I. Robertson Jr. wrote *Soldiers Blue and*

Gray (1988). Joseph T. Glatthaar, *The March to the Sea and Beyond: Sherman's Troops in the Savannah and Carolinas Campaigns* (1985) and Larry J. Daniel, *Soldiering in the Army of Tennessee: A Portrait of Life in a Confederate Army* (1991) discuss the soldiers in the western theater of the Civil War. Glatthaar's *Forged in Battle: The Civil War Alliance of Black Soldiers and White Officers* (1990), the earlier Benjamin Quarles's *The Negro in the Civil War* (1953), and Dudley T. Cornish's *The Sable Army: Negro Troops in the Union Army, 1861–1865* (1956) provide detailed information on black Union troops. A little known aspect of Civil War soldiering is discussed in Lauren M. Cook and DeAnne Blanton's *They Fought Like Demons: Women Soldiers in the Civil War* (2002), and Bonnie Tsui's *She Went to the Field: Women Soldiers of the Civil War* (2003).

An area of recurring interest regarding the Civil War soldier is motivation. Here, Gerald Linderman's *Embattled Courage: The Experience of Combat in the American Civil War* (1987) remains particularly important. Other books worth reading include: Michael Barton's *Goodmen: The Character of Civil War Soldiers* (1981), Reid Mitchell's *Civil War Soldiers: Their Expectations and Their Experiences* (1988) and *The Vacant Chair: The Northern Soldier Leaves Home* (1993), and Earl J. Hess's *The Union Soldier in Battle: Enduring the Ordeal of Combat* (1997). A good study of soldiers in one battle is: Joseph Allan Frank and George A. Reaves's *"Seeing the Elephant": Raw Recruits at the Battle of Shiloh* (1989).

Two particularly important recent books on the common soldier come from the pen of the leading Civil War historian of his generation, James M. McPherson. *What They Fought for, 1861–1865* (1994) and the Lincoln Prize winning *For Cause and Comrades, Why Men Fought in the Civil War* (1997) are an essential read for anyone wishing to gain insight into the experiences and thoughts of both Union and Confederate soldiers.

When he wrote the memoir reprinted here, Samuel Hankins did not overstate the accomplishment. His title a *Simple Story* expresses his feelings well. In truth, fighting in the Civil War as a common soldier was neither a simple task nor a forgettable experience. Hankins demonstrates this well in his meaningful memoir.

EXPLANATORY

Samuel Hankins, of Gulfport, Miss., has written a "Simple Story of a Soldier" which is appearing as a serial in the VET-ERAN and will be issued in book form. The title describes it with vivid accuracy. It teaches a lesson of army life and the horrors of war in a pathetic yet most ingenuous way. The reader will not tire of a sentence in it. Samuel W. Hankins is a native of Itawamba County, Miss., and served in the 2d Mississippi Infantry. The story is doubtless the most vivid record of a Confederate soldier's life that has been or will be written. He gives in detail the most ludicrous events as vividly as if a mature, gifted writer had kept a diary at the time, and his truly "simple story" will create sympathetic interest. It is so void of bitterness that a man who served on the "other side" will be as thoroughly interested, if possible, as his own comrades. He would sympathize with him in the hardships and privations of prison life and deplore that the government he served did not when it could render more humane service to him.——*From the Confederate Veteran.*

Simple Story of a Soldier

CHAPTER I

The spring loveliness of 1861 A.D. passed into summer un-
appreciated, for at that time excitement was widespread
with all classes throughout the whole of our Southland. Emi-
nent orators and others who had never before attempted
public address were proclaiming war by day and by night in
every city, town, and hamlet, together with the booming of
cannon and music by drum and fife as well as by brass bands.
Everybody was excited.

I had just entered my sixteenth year, and, like most boys
of my age, I felt my importance. At the first secession and
war meeting held in Guntown, where I lived, I was one of
the first to enlist, and was eager for the fray; but my father
(God bless his memory!) was bitterly opposed to secession,
although, unlike many who advocated war freely and after-
wards took no part therein, he enlisted early and served to

the end. Upon learning of my intention to enlist he said: "Why, my son, you are entirely too young to perform the duties that will be required of a soldier. And as I intend enlisting myself, you should remain at home to look after your dear mother and sisters while I am away. This war is going to be long and severe, and you will have ample time after you have grown older to do your share." I made no reply, as I was determined to enlist even without his consent. Upon learning of my determination he consented, which pleased me very much.

A full company of volunteers was raised in our little town and county. We were sworn into the Confederate service for twelve months. We then elected officers and a rush order was sent to Mobile, Ala., for uniforms and guns. We went into camp the following day and began to drill without waiting for our equipment. An open field was selected for a drill ground.

Our company numbered one hundred and eight. None of us, including officers, had any military training. The captain was a splendid man and well posted in civil matters, though ignorant as to military tactics. He was irritable by nature and vain. He would not appear on the drill ground in citizen's dress, but went about in search of a military suit and found one, although the like of it could be found nowhere else in America. The coat of unknown cut was bedecked with many large buttons and extra long epaulets, while the trousers were on the Zouave order. The hat was about two feet tall, with an additional height of ten or twelve inches of red, white, black, green, and blue feathers. The oldest citizen could not tell to what tribe or nation it had originally belonged. He also wore a sword, with a copy of Scott's "Military Tactics" protruding from his pocket.

On the following morning the company met at the place selected for our encampment. After organizing messes with from six to eight each and arranging our sleeping quarters, the captain ordered the company to assemble at the drill ground. On reaching the gate we passed through one by one, and were arranged against a plank fence in single file. This was done in order to get as straight a line as possible. After all had been lined up, the captain, arrayed as before described, took his position in front near its center and said: "Men, I will now proceed to instruct you in the first lessons of warfare." As he spoke he drew from his pocket Scott's "Tactics," which he opened and began to read aloud, telling the position of a soldier, how he should stand, etc. Then he began to read to us how we should move, and added: "Now, men, as I have fully explained to you the position of a soldier, I shall proceed to instruct you how you should march. When I give the command, 'Forward, march!' you must step off on your left foot, holding your bodies erect with your eyes cast slightly to the right. By so doing it will enable you to keep a straight line. Now, remember to step off on your left foot at the command, 'Forward, march!'"

There was about an equal division in left and right feet with us. "Hold on," said the captain; "that will never do. Go back to the fence again and we will try that over. Now remember, men, to step off on the left foot at the command, 'Forward, march!' "

The second time there was little if any improvement on the first. "Back against the fence, men!" said the captain. "Don't you know your left foot? Now be careful this time to step off on your left foot. Forward, march!"

It could be plainly seen from the captain's countenance that the third attempt was but little improvement on the second and that his temper was rising.

"Back against the fence, men! Now, I want you to understand me this time that when I say step off on your left foot I mean it and you must do so. When I say, 'Forward, march!' step off on your left foot. Now, don't forget this time to step off on the right foot. Forward, march!"

Three-fourths of the company poked out their right feet. "Hold on, you d— fools!" yelled the captain. "I meant the left foot was the right foot."

After several more efforts, we eventually moved off in fair order, the captain walking backward with book and sword in hand, repeating as he went, "Left foot, right foot, left foot, right foot; eyes to the right; left foot, right foot," and so on. After marching several yards, we on the left having kept our eyes entirely too much to the right had the captain about surrounded, when he backed against a small stump and fell over it flat on his back, his tall hat rolling several feet away, while his book and sword went in the opposite direction. This incident, of course, brought forth a yell from the entire company save the captain, who was in no mood for such a mishap, and he was not long in giving vent to his feelings. Thus ended our first attempt at drill.

On returning to our quarters the yelling had not subsided altogether, nor had the captain cooled to normal. He spoke seriously of resigning, though he was persuaded not to do so. He was excusable for his display of temper; for if there ever was an extreme test to try a man's patience, it is in drilling raw recruits.

CHAPTER II

Our general equipments arrived earlier than we expected. We were all anxious to be off to the war. Our uniforms, consisting of gray jackets, trousers, and caps, were very nice. We also drew knapsacks, haversacks, and cartridge boxes. Our guns were the old army muskets, though they looked new.

There has never lived a prouder boy than I when ordered into line for the first time fully equipped. The time for our departure was fixed; so on that day fathers, mothers, and all the kith and kin, including sweethearts far and near, gathered at the depot to bid us good-by. Many were the tears shed and many were the loved ones separated never to meet again. I seemed to be a target, being the youngest member of the company, and was given but little encouragement. Old men and women would say: "Good-by, my boy; we shall never see you any more." Little did I care whether I ever saw them again or not. I was headed for war and could not be bluffed off. Not a single tear did I shed, and I was astonished at the others for weeping. I expected that we would settle the matter to our liking and be at home in a few days.

The train that was to bear us away whistled, which brought forth more tears and more kissing. I was glad when the train moved away.

Corinth, Miss., was our first stopping place, as we were to meet there with nine other companies organized in North and East Mississippi to form a regiment. This was done the day following our arrival by electing field officers. The regiment became the 2d Mississippi Infantry. We were ordered at once to Harper's Ferry, Va., via the Memphis and Charleston Railroad. Freight cars were used principally in transporting troops. Every car, both inside and on top, was crowded with men, baggage, and boxes of provisions the like of which we saw no more.

My favorite place was on top of the car, where I could see and be seen. Many citizens gathered at the stations along the line to see the soldiers pass. Those who had tears to shed upon leaving home had now dried their eyes, and merry-making was in order. Speeches, some of which were ludicrous, were delivered from car doors and from the tops of cars at all stopping points. I recall a specimen delivered by a long, slim fellow from the top of a car, which I quote:

"Ladies and gentlemen, I have just left my home, my dear wife, and nine small children; also a very lucrative business, that of a crossroads saloon—all of which I gave up to battle for my country. It was like tearing my heartstrings to part from my dear ones, and especially my saloon."

The wag had neither wife, children, saloon, nor anything.

I was having a high old time until near Chattanooga, Tenn., when I noticed that our train was headed for a dark hole in the earth at the base of a mountain. I could plainly see that the hole was entirely too small for the train with me on top to pass through, and something had to be done, and done quickly. Down I went like a lizard on the running board, clinging to it by both hands with a deathlike grip. In a few moments we darted into the black and strangling smoke. I thought I had gone to the judgment before I had slain a single Yankee.

On our arrival at Harper's Ferry a brigade was formed of the following regiments: 2d and 11th Mississippi, 1st Tennessee, and 4th Alabama, with that gallant brigadier general, Bernard E. Bee, who a few months later fell at Bull Run, in command.

Here we got our satisfaction in drilling by brigade, regiment, company, and squad. We were drilled by Hardee's "Tactics," which contained many movements that were worthless in a fight. There is a vast difference between a soldier on dress parade and one in battle. In battle he has no time to see, if he can see, whether he is dressed right or left. About this time I had my first opportunity of testing my old musket. I was not at all acquainted with its character; though after the first command to fire, when I had recovered my courage, I wanted no further introduction. Why such a weapon was ever dealt us with which to fight the enemy is a puzzle to me, as there is about equal danger at either end. I was glad enough when I procured a good rifle from a dead Yankee.

Soldiers purchased, at twenty-five cents each, souvenirs said to have been of the rope and gallows used in the execution of John Brown. They were no doubt fraudulent.

When not at drill, the time was often spent in the vices of army life. A gambling epidemic broke out which spread with great rapidity, and but few escaped. I saw men give half their rations to have the other half cooked rather than stop gaming. All kinds of gambling were practiced. Morality for the time was ignored, and the soldier who endeavored to live right was ridiculed. If caught reading his Bible, such expressions were heard as, "Hello, parson; you must be scared. I don't think there will be any fighting soon;" or, "Hello, parson; what time do you expect to start a revival in camp?" Later on, however, serious thoughts of religion prevailed. When the shot and shell began to whiz by them, splintering rails and tearing off tree tops, with comrades falling around, they began to realize the great need of religion. One good battery with a good supply of grape shell holding an elevated position could bring hard-hearted sinners to repentance quickly. It did not require a good old sister to sit by and plead and fan with her turkey wing, begging him to repent of his sins. He was truly good then, but the great trouble was in keeping him so. If his life was spared, the sacred resolve would not long be remembered.

Often while on the march, when we would hear the

sound of cannon, comrades would say: "Boys, do you hear that?" Then after moving on nearer, when the cannonading became more frequent, you could hear: "Boys, we are going to get into it." Then there would begin the searching of pockets for gambling goods, playing cards especially. The thought of being killed with such in their pockets induced the soldiers to throw them away. The road would soon be covered with playing cards, dice, dice boxes, etc. Some would be slow in ridding themselves, although they would do so before entering battle. After the fight was over and all those who had passed through safely had gone into camp, every man not on duty could be found reading his Bible, except the few who could not read, and they were anxious to learn. Everything about camp would be as quiet as at the home of a good old Presbyterian on the Sabbath day.

This order of things lasted only a few days, however, when some fellow would slip around to the sutler's tent and purchase a new deck of cards, return to his quarters, pick up an oilcloth and spread it on the ground, open up his new deck, and begin to shuffle. Soon three or four others would step up, and a regular game of draw poker would begin. In less than a week the Bible-reading would be a thing of the past, when gambling generally would go on as before and would not stop until the next signal for a fight was heard in the front, when the same unloading would take place.

CHAPTER III

The army is about the only place where a man's character can be thoroughly analyzed. One might have a neighbor whom he had known from childhood and whom he thought he understood fully, when, after serving with him in the army for a few months, he would find out that the half had not been told. If there be a single good trait or damaging fault within, it will, like the measles, be sure to break out in the army. A mistaken idea prevailed among the people, including members of our company, as to who would make the best soldiers and what class of men could stand army life best. For instance, we had two members who were a holy terror at home and kept chips on their shoulders ready for a fracas at any time. All peaceable people were very polite to them in order to prevent a difficulty, and it was the general opinion that if the Confederacy could only muster up a few regiments of their kind the war would be of short duration. Those two fellows proved to be the only cowards we had. They could never be urged into battle, always claiming to be sick on such occasions. The only bugle call they learned was that for the sick. Any morning they could be seen moping up to the surgeon's quarters with pains in the back and hip and a dreadful taste in their mouths. They would not resent a gross insult given by the lowliest members. This was the case with such characters throughout the army. The most quiet and peaceable men at home were the best soldiers. Some crack shots at home who always returned from the woods with a dozen squirrels, each shot in the head, when in battle could not hit a "barn door" through excitement. The general opinion was that farmers, on account of the outdoor life to which they were accustomed, could stand the exposure of camp life best; but this was not always so.

All are familiar with the history of the battle of Bull Run, July 21, 1861; how we so greatly surprised the enemy and the result. The death of General Bee was our greatest loss. It was on that day that he proclaimed to his troops: "See Jackson's men standing like a stone wall."

In the most dangerous places something amusing quite frequently happened. A certain captain in our regiment had a great fondness for oratory. He would never let an opportunity pass for making a speech to his company. When we first fronted into line of battle and were awaiting orders, this captain, considering it a most opportune moment for addressing his men, began as follows: "Men, here you are for the first time in life drawn up in line of battle in front of a most bitter and damaging enemy, and one that does not only propose to rob you of your property but to deprive you of your constitutional rights and privileges for which your ancestors fought, bled, and died. Now, men, it behooves each of you to stand firm without dodging, and show them that you are a chip of the old block and will not submit to anything of the kind." Just then, boom! a shell burst overhead, scattering fragments here and there, while down went the captain flat on his face. He soon arose, nothing abashed, and continued his speech thus: "Yes, men, you must stand firm and not dodge." Boom! went the second shell, and down again went the captain. Rising again promptly, he continued: "Yes, men, to be dodging and showing any kind of fear will be placing a stigma upon your character and upon those loved ones at home which time can never erase." Boom! went the third shell, and down went the captain. On rising the third time he said with a grin: "But you may dodge the big ones if you like; it was the small ones I had reference to. I will finish my remarks when this thing is over."

Thomas B—, a member of our company, during the engagement wanted to know of the captain if he did not believe they would have to fall back soon. "I would not be surprised, Tom," replied the captain. "Well," Tom answered, "I had better start on now, as I am crippled."

Many have inquired of me as to how one felt on entering battle. Speaking for myself, at first it produced a feeling such as I could never explain, although my second entrance was one of dread. I have heard a few say that after one becomes accustomed to battle he will not dread it. There is no truth in this, and I believe all experienced soldiers dread it more and more after each experience. It is true, however, that after one gets squarely into an engagement, although comrades are falling thick and fast around him, the dread and fear are diminished and he forgets the danger.

One poor soldier was seen running for dear life, when a guard halted him and wanted to know why he was running. "They are jest a-fightin' over yonder!" exclaimed the soldier breathlessly. "Where are you going?" asked the guard. "I don't want to fight," said the soldier. Whereupon the guard ordered him back to the front, which he obeyed, although on starting back he was crying. The guard told him that he, a big, grown man, ought to be ashamed of crying like a baby. "I wish I was a baby," replied the soldier, "and a gal baby, too."

The first year of the war (1861) was a picnic compared to the three remaining years. We had good tents in which to quarter, plenty of clothing, with little marching and fighting to do; also we had plenty of rations and there was an excess of rice. I became so tired of rice that I have had no appetite for it since.

It was not until April, 1862, that the war began in earnest. It seemed that the commanders of both armies at that time came to the conclusion that maintaining armies was very expensive and that the issues must be forced.

We were stationed at that time on the heights south of the Rappahannock River, near Fredericksburg, Va., when orders were read to us on dress parade one evening to cook three days' rations, strike tents next morning by daylight, and be ready to move by sunrise. There was an unusually busy time in camp. At that period of the war every soldier had either a trunk or valise in connection with his knapsack, and every company had its tent, cooking utensils, and baggage wagons. In order to lighten my load I took from my knapsack and placed in my trunk everything except one change of underwear, one towel, a cake of soap, a comb, and a little book on how to cook fancy dishes—a thing that the Lord knows I had no need for. I also had two heavy blankets, a rug, a knapsack, three days' rations, a heavy gun, and a cartridge box containing forty rounds of ammunition—a good load for a broncho. I placed my trunk in one of the baggage wagons. When all was in readiness, the bugle sounded for us to fall into line. There was a heavy cloud, and just as our orderly sergeant finished calling the roll the cloud seemed to split wide open, and such a downpour of water I had never seen. Almost drowned, and notwithstanding that the deluge continued, we moved off. When we reached the lowlands, a distance of about one mile, we found all the small streams overflowing, and those not bridged had to be forded. Frequent heavy showers continued, and we were drenched.

After some three miles' march, my rug weighed about fifty pounds, so I decided to drop it. A few hundred yards farther on I abandoned one of my blankets and a little later my knapsack. I knew I had plenty of clothing in my trunk, so I felt easy. Here let me state, however, that when I threw away my knapsack I lost the last change of underwear, the last towel, the last cake of soap, and my comb. My garments remained on me until they wore off, except for some sun-shiny days when on the bank of some stream they were taken off and washed. What became of the wagon with my trunk I have not found out up to the present time. Fifty years have come and gone since I began looking for it. I was not alone. What became of the thousands of blankets and clothing thrown away that day?

The road was worked into a very soft mortar bed ankle deep, and rain was still falling. It was fearful. One member of our company while attempting to cross a bad place on a log fell full length into the mud. Some one asked him how he felt. He replied that he regretted only one thing, which was that he did not drown.

The adage that politeness is the cheapest and best-paying investment which one can make is no doubt true, but it is at times inconvenient. Gen. Joseph E. Johnston, then in com-mand of the Army of Northern Virginia, was passing from the rear to the front. As soon as he appeared the soldiers began cheering him all along the line. Through politeness and to show his appreciation of the ovation given him he pulled off his cap and rode with it in his hand for miles, while the rain was pelting down on his sleek bald head.

CHAPTER IV

I now began to consider seriously the advice that my dear father had given me which, if I had followed it, would have spared me this bitter pill.

We pulled along miserably through the mud and rain until after dark, when we halted for the night, stacking arms on the roadside. The distance we had gone that day was estimated at thirty miles. None of the wagons containing our tents had arrived; and as there was no attempt made to start a fire, not a light was to be seen anywhere. We were so completely worn out that after partaking of a few bites of hardtack and boiled beef we searched for places to sleep. I found some drifted leaves near, and, unrolling my wet blanket, I spread it out and got on it in my soaked condition, covering my head and ears and using my cartridge box for a pillow. Notwithstanding that the rain still poured, I was soon asleep, and did not wake until the bugle sounded for roll call the next morning.

When I got up I found, to my horror, that our company had occupied an old abandoned graveyard, and I had slept full length in a sunken grave. I could not have been persuaded to sleep there had I known the surroundings, having been reared with ghost-telling darkies. Many a night had I sat in a split-bottom chair in Uncle Sam's cabin and listened to an old darky's dreadful stories. When my mother called me to go to bed, Uncle Sam had to go with me to the house, and once in bed I covered my head tight. The impression made then remains with me still.

Soon our company was on the move again, with but little change in the weather. The road we traversed was said to be the one that Washington had gone over *en route* to Yorktown, and it must have been from its old, worn appearance. Pulling along as we had done the day previous, I became a full-grown prodigal before many hours passed, and gladly would I have returned to my father's house if such a privilege had been allowed me. I never let them know at home about my hardships; I was too proud. We marched about the same distance that day and slept under wet blankets.

The next morning we found that our scanty third day's rations had soured and were unfit for use. We threw them all away and started out on empty stomachs. The weather had now changed to a slow, drizzling rain. Soon I grew very hungry. When night came, the outlook for rations was poor, and we stacked arms hopelessly. However, in about an hour the joyful call, "Come and draw your rations," was heard, and there was no delay. The rations consisted of one cup of flour, one pound of beef, and a tablespoonful of salt. Then the question arose as to how we were going to prepare the flour. We had no cooking utensils of any kind. Some enterprising fellow discovered that by cutting through the bark of the green hickory tree it would peel off and answer for a tray; so after mixing the flour, salt, and cold water, we soon had our dough in the shape of snakes which we twisted around our gun rods and stuck in the ground in front of the fire, changing front to rear occasionally. Bread cooked in this way had to be eaten hot, if at all, so we had no bread for breakfast.

We had one instinctive business man in our company, Billie McC., who seemed to realize the importance of having a skillet, and he secured a nice light one, made some straps, and when on the move strapped it on his back where he had once worn his knapsack. Much fun was poked at Billie and his skillet, which he took good-naturedly; but he hung on to the skillet, and at night would sleep with it under his head. No one dared to take issue with Billie upon any subject for fear of offending him and being denied the loan of the skillet. Soon the cooking utensils dwindled down to that one skillet, which sixty-five or seventy men had to use. It was never allowed to cool. Billie took it to his Mississippi home, and some of the boys said that he had it at his marriage some months after the war closed, and had the officiating clergyman add an additional obligation that the bride would not only honor and obey him, but that she would be careful of that skillet.

The sun rose bright the next morning for the first time since leaving Fredericksburg. We moved off, but only a short distance, when we halted and stacked arms in the vicinity of Yorktown. Thus ended what I consider the most disagreeable march of the war. True, we had some tough, cold, and forced marches, but they were not so severe. We soon unrolled our blankets, spreading them in the sunshine, and we stood in the sun so as to dry our clothes.

About noon the wagons arrived and we arranged to live in more comfort. Just then we were startled by a volley of musketry all along our front, and we were quickly ordered into line. I had not been feeling well, though the excitement caused me to forget my condition. A detail of two or three was made from each company to remain and guard the camp. To this detail were handed by those in line watches, pocketbooks, and finger rings, with instructions as to whom the articles were to be sent in case the owner was killed. We remained in line a few moments, expecting to be ordered to advance. Soon the firing ceased, and it was found to be a false alarm caused by some foolish picket firing at an imaginary enemy. We were ordered to break ranks and return to our quarters.

The next morning found me with a high fever and the measles well broken out. About ten o'clock a couple of my

messmates assisted me to an open-top wagon to be sent to
the hospital at Richmond. The wagon contained only one
other person, a little Virginian, who also had measles. We had
room to lie down in the wagon, where my comrades spread
out my blanket and bade me good-by. We started off in the
direction of Williamsburg, but had not proceeded far when
it began to rain, and continued the remainder of the day.
Having no protection, both of us got soaking wet. I had often
heard it said that it was sure death to get wet with measles,
and I felt very uneasy.

We reached Williamsburg at dark, and our driver assisted
us into an old vacant house, where he left us to shift for ourselves. That house must have been built a century before, as
the moss was three or four inches thick over the leaky roof
and hanging all around the building at the eaves from four
to six feet long.

The next morning our driver returned and assisted us
into his wagon. In a short time we were at a landing on the
James River and helped aboard a boat that was bound for
Richmond. On our arrival there we were conducted to a fish
cart propelled by an old mule and driven by an ex-convict.
I wanted to know of him our destination, and he replied:
"The hospital."

After jolting us around some eight or ten blocks, we
halted in front of an old tobacco factory that had been converted into a so-called hospital, though it had more the appearance of a morgue, as there was on each side of the main

entrance a stack of plain coffins of various lengths that extended to the second windows. Surely, thought I, they did
not send us to such a place to be nursed back to health!

My little friend and I were consigned to Ward 4. The number I shall never forget. That ward contained eighty cots, all
occupied save the two for my friend and myself which had
been that morning vacated by death.

The officials and nurses, all of whom had been detailed
from the army, received us cordially. The steward then came
to enroll us. After giving him my full name, company, regiment, and brigade, he wanted to know what county in Mississippi I was from. I told him Itawamba. After surveying me
for a few moments, he remarked that I had no business in
the army; that I had better be back home attending school.

The second night after our arrival my little friend passed
away and was placed in one of the boxes that we saw at the
front entrance. I decided that my box required another day's
seasoning. Every morning the hospital undertaker with his
measuring pole would visit each ward to get the measure of
those who had died during the night. There would always be
from five to six taken out. One poor fellow was sleeping
on his back with both eyes open, having all the appearance
a dead man, when the undertaker in taking his measure
woke the poor fellow, who was frightened half to death. He
jumped up, yelling, "I am not dead! I am not dead!" knocking
the undertaker's measure winding.

I remained there about ten days and left at the first
chance, fully determined that if they ever attempted to send

me to another hospital they would have to tie me, and I would squeal like a hog all the way.

Our brigade had moved from Yorktown nearly to Richmond during the time I was confined at the hospital, so I had to go only a short distance upon returning to find it. I reached there just in time for the battle of Seven Pines. That battle was more of an artillery engagement than one with small arms on our part of the line. We supported our battery, one of the most dangerous of positions. I had rather charge two batteries than support one. In the latter case you are as helpless as a babe, awaiting orders when it appears that everybody and everything are trying to murder you. It is true that we had the privilege of lying down, which is some protection if in an open field; but if the engagement is in timber, soldiers are in greater danger of being crushed by falling tree tops. The enemy fell back into another position, and our battery moved up to where they commanded a new and more lively engagement.

While passing over the ground evacuated by the enemy Thomas B., a member of our company, picked up a Northern newspaper. Now, Tom was not a fellow to shirk duty by any means; for, like myself and many others, he was a great fighter on leaving home, but had by this time cooled down to the opinion that all such matters should be settled by arbitration. After reaching our position, we were ordered down. Tree tops and branches were falling thick and fast, with grapeshot and fragments of shells whizzing in every direction. After cannonading had been going on for some time,

Tom raised his head and said to Jim C., who was also of our company and noted for being the best reader we had, "Jim, O Jim!" (you had to talk loud to be heard at all in that uproar) and Jim yelled, "What is it, Tom?" he too having his face to the earth like the rest. "I wish you would look in this d— Yankee paper and see whether peace negotiations are on hand or not." "Tom, this ain't any place for reading newspapers," said Jim. We all had to smile at Tom's request in spite of our serious surroundings.

CHAPTER V

After the battle of Seven Pines we went into camp near Richmond, where we remained a few days, when our brigade was sent to Stonewall Jackson, in the Shenandoah Valley. This trip was made by rail from Richmond to Staunton via Lynchburg. It required three long trains of box and flat cars to move us. The train that contained our regiment and a few additional companies, comprising fifteen hundred men, was propelled by two engines.

At Farmville, Va., we came to the noted long and tall bridge. This bridge had been reported unsafe, and the traveling public between Richmond and Lynchburg would go through Danville, Va., many miles out of the way, to avoid it. We had to risk it, though; and knowing about its being condemned, I had been dreading the danger for some time. I was on top of the car (my usual place) when we arrived at the bridge, and when near its center the train came to a standstill. I looked over the edge of the car far down into the valley, where cattle grazing looked as small as sheep. The engines began to puff and blow and slip, then a slack was followed by a quick jerk, when it seemed that the frail structure was giving way and sinking beneath me. This slacking and jerking lasted one hour, though it appeared to last longer than the war (four years). Conjectures were rife as to the cause of the delay. It was my greatest fright during the war. However, we passed over in safety.

On reaching Staunton we left the railroad and marched down the valley a few miles, where we found Jackson's command. We went into camp just at the foot of the Shenandoah Mountains, where we received orders to cook three days' rations. The next morning we moved across the valley direct for the Blue Ridge. Crossing it, we went in a reverse direction. In a few days we were down on the Peninsula in the rear of McClellan's army.

Before we left Richmond for the valley a young man, Joseph Crompton, attached himself to our company and was received into our mess. Joe was a most noble fellow, handsome and polite. He had been reared by wealthy parents who had both died, leaving him a considerable fortune. Money had not spoiled him, as is often the case, and we greatly respected him. He had just graduated from Emory and Henry College (in June, 1862), winning the first prize in oratory, and came direct from school to the army.

On the morning of June 28, while we were seated on the

ground eating breakfast, each one from his scanty haversack, some one remarked that he was expecting a fight that day, and two or three others concurred. "Well," said Joe, "if we do have a fight, I am going in, though I will not get a shot." When we expressed our surprise at his remark, he steadily held to the conviction that he would be killed before he got a shot. "Do you really feel that way?" two or three asked. "I do," he replied solemnly. "Well, I wouldn't go in then," said one. "Yes," said Joe; "if there is a fight, I am going in, though it will be just as I have said."

About ten o'clock that morning a lively skirmish opened up some distance in our front. We were ordered to double-quick forward. There was a skirt of timber with much undergrowth through which we had to pass, which caused breaks in the line, as we were marching by fours. The day was hot; our water had given out and none was available. We reached an old-fashioned rail fence which we tore down and entered a large level field. Beyond this field was another skirt of timber, which was occupied by the enemy, where the fighting was going on. Just as we were to charge, our first lieutenant in command (the captain was in the hospital) turned around with his back to the enemy and said: "Close up, men; I had rather fight than to double-quick this way." We were about out of breath, and just as he uttered these words I heard something like the noise of a rock thrown against a plank. Then I saw the lieutenant fall forward. He was shot in the back of the head and killed instantly.

After entering the field, we had changed from double-quick to quick time, and had gone about twenty yards when Joe said to me: "Let's drop our tin cups; they are so much in the way." I was next to the fence and Joe just to my left. Just then, bang! a similar sound to that when the lieutenant fell, and Joe Crompton fell forward on his face. I made an effort to catch him, but failed. There was no other way to pass except by stepping over his head and shoulders. As I did so I heard him groan, and I saw a stream of blood about the size of my finger shooting up through his black hair. I wanted to stop with him, but I knew he was dead and there was nothing I could do. Thus passed away one of our best young men. I never regretted anything more than his death.

We moved on some three or four hundred yards, halted, and came to a front, when Gen. W. C. Whiting, commanding our brigade, gave the order, "Come on!" (not go on). He was seated on his spirited dapple gray. We gave the Rebel yell and across that field we rushed, while men were falling thick and fast. Our orderly sergeant was killed and our second lieutenant wounded. Our third lieutenant being on detached duty, our second sergeant took command of the company. For a while the enemy was very stubborn; but evidently learning that it was Stonewall Jackson after them, they made a break. We pressed them for some distance to the top of a hill overlooking a small valley, where we halted and ceased firing, as the smoke and dust were so dense that we could scarcely see at all. When it had cleared, we noticed down the valley to our right many of the enemy moving out rapidly. They had thrown away their arms and baggage and were making good their escape, though in front of us on the hill across the valley they had succeeded in checking their men to some extent.

In a few minutes a balloon ascended containing a man whom they had sent to make observations. The balloon was attached to a long rope, and as soon as it had ascended as far as the rope would admit, it seemed to come to a perfect standstill. Just then Captain Riley, commanding our brigade battery at the time, had his guns in position and ordered a shot at the balloon. Hundreds of us witnessed it, and I venture to say that no better artillery shot was made during the war. The shell exploded just between the car and basket containing the man and the balloon, and out tumbled the poor fellow.

Not longer than three years ago I was passing along the street in front of a hotel in Columbus, Miss., where some gentlemen were sitting out in front talking. As I came near I heard an old gray-haired gentleman remark that one of his men was shot out of a balloon during the war. This caused me to halt. I said to him: "My friend, did not that happen at Gaines's Farm, Va., during the Seven Days' Battle?" "It did," said he. "Well," I replied, "would you believe it when I tell you that I was within fifty feet of the cannon that made the shot? Was the man killed?" "He was," he replied, "and was a member of my company." Then we had a long and very pleasant conversation.

Well, we had no more fighting that day, and remained in line where we first halted until about dark, when we fell back one hundred yards or more into an open field for the night. Our company had entered the fight with seventy-six men. When we halted on top of the hill, there were only sixteen of us left. The second sergeant was in command. Many of the missing ones had broken down from the long distance double-quicked in the heat and without water.

That night we were ordered to remain in line, and no one was to break it. I know it was the most miserable night of my life. The cry of the wounded for help and for water could be heard in every direction by both armies, and no help or water could we give. My own thirst was unspeakable torture. I had not had a drop of water since nine o'clock that morning. My tongue was swollen. Gladly would I have risked my life for a drink had I known where to find it. To add to the discomfort, we were cold to freezing. It was one of those hot days in June followed by a cold night.

At daybreak we moved off in the direction the enemy had taken. We could hardly avoid stepping on the dead, so thickly were they strewn; many had died during the night. Some lay on their backs with one arm uplifted as if signaling for help. About eight o'clock we came to a small creek containing holes of stagnant water which we drank eagerly and gratefully.

CHAPTER VI

On the second day after Gaines's Farm we captured a fort without the loss of a man or a round of ammunition. The enemy had built the fort and were strongly fortified at White Oak Swamp. Gen. Stonewall Jackson fooled them by coming up behind. As soon as they learned of his approach they began in haste to get out, and crossed the swamp in front of their works, the way they were expecting us. After that they had a long hill to climb, and their teams could not move as fast as they wished with their heavy loads of ammunition, army supplies, and cannon. They spiked their cannon, knocked their teams in the head with pole axes, and set fire to their wagons. Some threw away their guns, knapsacks, and blankets, making good their escape. As we passed across the swamp and reached the hill in pursuit we found the road blockaded with dead horses and mules, burnt wagons, spiked cannon, blankets, knapsacks, guns, etc. Lead had melted and covered the roadbed with one solid sheet.

Our next engagement was at Malvern Hill. The day before it took place I was detailed to serve on outside picket duty. Our line extended two or three miles, a portion being through an old field covered with large scrubby pines, with no undergrowth. We were stationed about one hundred yards apart, with instructions usually given outside pickets—i. e., at the approach of the enemy to fire and fall back. My post was within the old field. From our line we could hear the enemy giving orders and their bands playing. After I had been on post about an hour, I heard the cough of a horse in front of me. I stooped so as to see under the low branches of the pines, and saw the legs of two horses, also those of a man on each horse, and they were coming my way. I thought I would withhold my instructions a few moments so as to see more plainly, they being some distance off and moving with difficulty under the low branches. After I could see better, I saw that they were dressed in gray. They came on directly to where I was standing, and it was General Jackson and a lone courier. I presented arms. The General politely returned the salute, spoke not a word, bowed his head in passing under a limb, and went on. What could he have been doing so near the enemy with only a single courier?

In the Malvern Hill engagement another disagreeable duty was the supporting of a battery. General McClellan, commanding the Federal forces, occupied the Turkey Bend on James River, where he had many gunboats and transports.

He seemed to have concentrated all his field artillery within the bend after dark that night and turned the entire thing, including gunboats, upon us. They completely silenced our batteries, as they had so many more, including the large guns and mortars on their gunboats, the mortars pitching over those "wash pots," while the large guns were throwing long shells. The firing was terrific, though they failed in locating our lines, overshooting us all the time. In our rear there was the appearance of thousands of large bursting skyrockets. Not a man in our regiment was hurt. While the heaviest firing was going on we were in a skirt of woods much nearer them than they supposed. At one time the command, "Attention!" was passed along our line. We were all seated on the ground, but were soon on our feet. I felt that if we had to charge all that racket certain death would come to every one of us. We stood in line some time, expecting to be ordered to advance; but as we were not, we resumed our seats. I sat down by a small pine bush, my back against it, my gun across my knees, and was soon asleep. At what time the cannonading ceased I had no knowledge, as I did not awaken until daylight, when I found the enemy all gone and everything perfectly still. All the while that that great waste of ammunition had been going on General McClellan was loading his transports with his men and sending them down the river to avoid capture.

After the Seven Days' Battle we moved up near Richmond, where we remained a few weeks, until General Lee started on his expedition into Maryland, when the battle of

Sharpsburg was fought. Our company's loss in that engagement was small, only two killed and five wounded, our captain losing a leg.

We had politics in the army just as we have in civil life. The appointing powers had their pets, and many incompetent men were chosen. A member of a certain regiment said to me that his colonel appointed his wife's brother, who had never had any experience in human surgery, as surgeon of his regiment. He was only a veterinary surgeon, and before the was confined his practice exclusively to cattle. He said further that one of their men was run over accidentally by an artillery wagon, having his legs dislocated, when this so-called surgeon attempted to reset them and made an awful botch of it. We had many men holding "bombproof" positions who should have been in the ranks. Almost any crossroads butcher could amputate a limb, but it required a capable surgeon to save one. I will say in justice to the dead that our regiment, the 2d Mississippi, was fortunate in having one of the best colonels in the army, and who after the war for years made one of the best Governors the State of Mississippi ever knew— John M. Stone. He was a man who had no pets in the army or out of it. The result was that we had a surgeon who understood his business.

After the battle of Sharpsburg we recrossed the Potomac River into Virginia, going up the Shenandoah Valley to within four miles of Winchester, where we went into camp and remained for several weeks. The weather was growing cold with considerable frost, when we were ordered to Richmond again. On our march thence we reached the North Fork River a short distance from where it emptied into the Shenandoah. The river was not deep but wide, and it had to be forded. Many pulled off their trousers and shoes, while others did not. The water was very swift, and we felt as if our legs were being sawed off.

After crossing this river we went not quite a mile when we came to the Shenadoah, a much wider and deeper stream, which had to be forded also. Here one poor fellow put his gun down by a tree while he pulled off his trousers and shoes. These he rolled up into a bundle, placed it on his shoulder, and crossed, entirely forgetting his gun. After reaching the opposite side of the river, he remembered the gun; and knowing that it would have to be accounted for, he stored his trousers and shoes in an ambulance near by while he recrossed. Securing his gun, he returned to find that the ambulance had moved off with his clothes. The poor fellow struck out at double-quick time in pursuit with his bare feet and legs, while the cold morning's breeze was fluttering the lower end of his short army shirt and every soldier was yelling at him as he passed along. The yelling could be heard for a mile or more.

We remained in Richmond only a few days. Our brigade was then composed of the following regiments: 2d, 11th, 42d Mississippi, and 55th North Carolina, commanded by Gen. Joe R. Davis. We were ordered down to Black Water River, in the direction of Suffolk, Va., the enemy having sent out a house- and bridge-burning force from that place. On reaching the river we found that they had just burned the bridge, and smoke was ascending above the tree tops from the farm dwellings that they had fired across the river. Our pontoon corps soon had a bridge over which we crossed, although the enemy made their way back to Suffolk without showing fight. After establishing a strong picket post, we re-crossed the river and went into camp. The following morning we began to fortify. It was the latter part of October and quite cool. When not at work on our fort and rifle pits, we were busy building huts in which to quarter, as we had no tents and had been without them for months. Only field officers were entitled to them, including quartermasters, commissaries, and surgeons.

In a week or two after our arrival violent smallpox broke out in camp. Not a single case that I knew about recovered. Billie Shackfoot, my messmate and bunkmate, was quite sick one entire night with a high fever. In the morning I obtained permission to search for some milk for him, which was a hard task. I was gone two or three hours, and on my return I found that they had moved him to the pesthouse, where he died in two days. For some time I was depressed and anxious, as I had slept with him.

All our work was of but little service, as the enemy had sent out another bridge- and house-burning force from Newbern, N. C., to Nance River, near Goldsboro, where they burned the public and railroad bridges about a mile south of the town. Our command was ordered there to intercept them. We made the move by railroad, reaching Goldsboro about sunset. The evening was quite cold, as it was late in November. We were ordered from the cars into line at once. Several were without shoes and thinly dressed, and I was of that class. Owing to the extreme cold, all without shoes were excused and stepped out of line except myself. I had heard it said while in camp that certain ones threw away their shoes in order to be excused from going into battle, and I was determined not to be classed with them; so I marched off with the command to meet the enemy, which was reported in force on the opposite side of the river.

It was dark when we reached the burnt bridge; but we soon had our pontoon ready, on which we crossed, and had gone a short distance when the regiments filed to the right and left of the public road into the swamp and fronted into line of battle, with orders for no one to speak above a whisper. After standing in line a while, most of us sat down.

I was very cold. I had my only blanket rolled around my neck and shoulders. I would not unroll it, as we were expecting to be engaged at any moment. Soon I was asleep. Our scouts reported that the enemy had fallen back toward Newbern. When attention was called and others arose, I remained asleep. One of my comrades noticed this, so he pulled at me until he had me on my feet. As soon as he turned me loose I dropped to the ground again. Seeing that I could not stand alone, one comrade on each side of me assisted me along until we had recrossed the river, when I had gotten up enough circulation to walk alone. Had we remained in line thirty minutes longer, I am satisfied that I would have frozen to death.

We then marched into a large forest of tall long-leaf pine timber, with scarcely any undergrowth. Here we stacked arms. There was much pine straw which we raked up for bedding. Two others and I formed a partnership, each having a blanket. We spread one on the straw, while we covered with the other two, using our cartridge boxes as head rests. It was between ten and eleven o'clock when we laid down. We covered up head and ears and were soon asleep. I had the most comfortable position, the middle, and I slept well.

The next morning I was the first of the three to awaken. I reached up to uncover my head, when snow filled my face. There had been a six-inch fall of snow after we had retired. The whole forest as far as I could see resembled a well-filled cemetery (only lacking order), and their coming out of those little snow-covered mounds was well worth seeing. Some one remarked that he imagined it would appear that way on the final day when the graves give up their dead. There was not a tent to be seen; field officers shared the same as privates that night. Not a stick of dry timber was there with which to build a fire. My two bedfellows suggested that, as I had no shoes and they had, I remain under cover while they went in search of fuel. They returned soon with fence rails. We cleared away the snow and soon had a fire. Although my body felt the heat, my bare feet suffered in the melting snow and were frostbitten, from which I have ever since suffered.

The sun came out bright and the wind shifted to the south. That day there was a general snowballing, regiments against each other. One man was killed during the frolic, being struck with some hard substance. I was in no condition to participate.

CHAPTER VII

We received orders to cook three days' rations, which signified that a move was on hand. However, we did not move. A similar order was given some days later; and as we still did not move, we began to fell those long pine trees and split slats and boards for shanties against the bad weather. The timber was the best that could have been found for the purpose. Streets were laid off, and in less than four days we had a city of about three thousand males. Some flexible bush or vine was used in fastening the framework, as there were no nails in the army. All the time we were working I did all that I could in my bare feet.

A few days after completing our quarters a member of our company who was wounded and had been at home on furlough returned. He brought with him a full suit of good woolen clothing, also underwear and a pair of homemade shoes and socks that my dear mother had sent me. Everything except the shoes had been made by her own hands. It was indeed a happy surprise, as I was not expecting anything of the kind. During the war I never asked for anything from home. Having left without the consent of my parents, I wanted to show them what an independent, resolute son they had, and I did so completely.

Instead of moving on, as we expected, we remained where we stacked arms that night of the snow until the 1st of April following. The unused tree tops made excellent firewood, though the black smoke made every one look like he had just prepared himself to appear on the stage to sing "Shoo, Fly! Don't Bother Me."

Our rations during the entire stay consisted of only unsifted corn meal and very poor beef. Only on two occasions were we issued a day's ration of flour. Each sergeant would throw all the beef belonging to his mess into a large camp kettle and boil it down, leaving two or three inches of water, or gravy, as we called it. In this we dipped our unsifted corn bread; so the one who ate the most bread ate the most bran. There was not a sifter in the camp. This diet proved wholesome; we all fattened on it and had the very best health.

About the 1st of April we were ordered to join General Longstreet, near Suffolk, Va. This move was made by rail a portion of the way and the remainder overland. The enemy had been in possession of Suffolk for several months, and had felled every tree for at least a mile west of the city. They had built forts and had dug rifle pits that extended across the west side of the town. The timber cut was mostly scrub pine, and the entire area was a mass of tree stumps. We reached the western vicinity of Suffolk an hour or so before sunset and went into camp. I rushed back to meet our cooking utensil wagon to try to be the first to get the skillet allowed our company.

I had gone perhaps a mile when I noticed a man with a skillet on his head walking very fast toward me and occupying the middle of the road. When near enough, I noticed that he was the hardest-looking specimen I had ever met. His hair was long, his beard heavy and unkempt, his eyes badly crossed, and he had unusually long arms and legs. He also stammered badly in his speech, which I learned soon. He could have played the wild man to perfection at a side show. I stepped aside to give him the right of way, and as I did so I ventured to ask him to what regiment he belonged. He halted suddenly, half about faced, and, holding out at arm's length his skillet, or spider, as it was called by some, began: "I-I belong to the fif-fif-fifth Nor-North Carolina. Now, ca-call m-m-me T-T-Tarheel, d— you, a-a-and I-I will k-knock you in t-the head with this spider." To have called him a Tarheel would have been the last act of my life, and the fright he had given me was next to my railroad fright on that bridge at Farmville. Soon I met our wagon, although I missed the skillet. The driver told me that one of the company had taken it before starting on the march that morning.

On returning I found that I had been selected on a detail of six men from each company for picket duty that night at nine o'clock to remain until nine the next night. We were issued one hundred rounds of ammunition each. Between eight and nine o'clock we moved to the edge of the cut timber, taking spades and shovels. Our scouts had captured their outside pickets, so we had nothing to do but creep through the underbrush to within rifle range of their pits, where we deployed into squads of three some twenty-five yards apart, each squad digging a pit about thirty inches deep, and wide and long enough to accommodate three men, the dirt being thrown in front.

At daylight firing began all along the line, and there was a regular bang! bang! the entire day. Several were killed by exposing themselves foolishly, one from our pit. At one time a very large eagle was soaring high about midway between the lines when firing began at the king of birds. Hundreds of shots were made before he was brought down between the lines, there to remain uncalled for by either side.

This picket duty was kept up nearly the entire month of April. When not raining, the service was not so bad, except for the uncomfortable feeling of being cramped up for twenty-four hours in succession. On two or three occasions the hard rains would nearly fill our pits with water. We would bail it out with our caps, though we had to sit with our feet in water most of the time. Why this movement I never knew, as there was never any effort made to capture the place.

We left Suffolk about the 1st of May on a quick march. The enemy had sent out a force in the direction of Black Water River. General Longstreet ordered our brigade to intercept them. We started about dark with orders not to speak above a whisper and not to shun the water. The country was low, flat, and sandy, and there were many ponds in the road deep and long through which we had to wade. We marched all night at quick step without a single halt with wet shoes filled with sand and skinned feet. We reached our old quarters and fortifications at Black Water about eight o'clock in the morning, ahead of the enemy. The distance traveled was said to be forty-five miles. The enemy made no attempt to cross the river.

The third day after our arrival Colonel Stone took a canvass of his regiment for a volunteer to sit on a horse all night about one-fourth of a mile in advance of the outside picket post. Such duty was not compulsory and had to be a voluntary act, for which I had a perfect fondness. On reaching our company the colonel wanted to know of our captain if he had a man who would volunteer to perform that duty. The captain's answer was that he didn't know whether he had a man that would do so or not, but he had a boy who would; so I was called and told what was wanted. I jumped at the proposition like a trout for a live minnow. The horse given me, a fine, spirited animal, belonged to our lieutenant.

About dark I was conducted to my post of duty on the main road that ran through the swamp on the opposite side of the river from the camp. It was low and flat, covered with white sand. From my post I could see several hundred feet. There was no possible chance for the enemy to flank me, as on both sides there was a perfect jungle of vines, briers, and

water. It was said that many wild animals, such as cata-
mounts, wildcats, and a few panthers, inhabited the swamp;
so there I was left, with my rifle across the pommel of my
saddle, with instructions to fire at the approach of the enemy
and fall back as fast as the horse could travel to the picket
line, so as to give them time to be in readiness.

My horse soon became restless, tramping about, snort-
ing, and pawing up the earth. The mosquitoes and gnats being bad, I soon found out that I was in for it. Several times
during the night I could hear, or imagine so, the snarl of
some ferocious animal or see the enemy approaching; while
the little frogs were calling, "John Brown, John Brown,"
and the bullfrogs were saying, "He's drunk, he's drunk," all
through one of the longest nights of my life. At sunrise I was
relieved, fully satisfied with volunteering.

We remained at that point only a week or two, during which time occurred the saddest event of the war in
the death of Stonewall Jackson. He was our favorite commander, and I had never until then entertained any doubt as
to our final success, for in him we had implicit faith. Many
tears were shed on that dark day.

CHAPTER VIII

Our next move was up the Rappahannock River near Fredericksburg, where we were attached to General Heth's division, A. P. Hill's corps, and did picket duty along the banks of the river until General Lee began his move the latter part of June into the enemy's country. On this move we forded the Potomac River. It was rather wide, but only about waist deep at the time. The water, however, was swift. The river bed was very rough and slippery, so that wading was extremely difficult. Many got a ducking, to the great amusement of those who escaped. The artillery and wagons and those on horseback had to cross about a hundred yards below us. Some officer seated on his horse about midway the river was yelling at us to close up, when his horse stumbled and he went over the horse's head foremost into the water. An uproar by the soldiers followed his catastrophe. Our own brigade was the second to cross. Looking back after reaching the opposite side, we saw the army, miles in length, winding its way through the mountains like a huge snake down into the river. It was a grand sight.

Our first night in camp in Maryland was in the vicinity of Hagerstown. I was on provost duty that night, which was to keep the soldiers out of town. We made only a few arrests. The reason we had so little trouble was that General Lee had issued very stringent orders about molesting private property and committing depredations, and his men well understood him.

Hagerstown was strongly Union in sentiment, so all along the streets could be heard female voices singing Northern airs and war songs; but they had nothing that could compare with "Dixie."

The next morning, while the army was passing through the town and before we were relieved from duty, General Lee appeared. The female population nearly went wild over him. All along the street through which he passed there was a perfect wringing of hands with these exclamations, "O what a grand man he is!" and "Don't you wish he was ours?"

That night we camped in Pennsylvania just over the line. As we marched along the next day we found most of the homes abandoned, the owners having fled to the mountains. Some in their haste to depart had not even closed their doors, leaving everything exposed. Nothing was molested by our men. I did not see the smoke going up from a single dwelling or any other building fired by our men while in the

enemy's country. The citizens expected it by way of retalia-
tion. Our army took only food for man and beast and ex-
changed old army mules for their large, overgrown horses.
This was a mistake, as one mule is worth a dozen horses for
military service.

On the night of June 30 we bivouacked on the summit of
a high mountain, during which a heavy rain fell, drenching
us. The following morning we marched down from the
mountain to the pike that led to Gettysburg and then on in
that direction.

Between nine and ten o'clock on July 1 we halted at the
foot of a hill and fronted, when our colonel (Stone) came
down the line, stopping in front of each company and giving
instructions. On reaching ours he remarked: "Men, clean
out your guns, load, and be ready. We are going to have it!"
Our first lieutenant, Whitley, had been under arrest a few
days for disobeying some petty order and had kept along
with the company at will. To him the colonel remarked:
"Lieutenant Whitley, you can take command." "Thank you,
Colonel," said Whitley, obeying. We then marched to the top
of the hill.

Up to this time not a report of a gun of any kind had we
heard that morning.

Other regiments filed to the left until Heth's Division was
all in line except the 11th Mississippi, which was on detached
duty. In front of the entire line there was a large opening
descending into a small valley, and across this up a slope to
the edge of a line of timber. The entire opening appeared to

be covered with wheat ready for harvest. To our left we could see a long way down the valley, though to our right only a short distance could be seen on account of hills. Twenty or thirty paces in front of us Bradford's Mississippi Battery had unlimbered and been placed in line. Just as we came to a front I noticed one of the gunners directly in front of me lean backward (as did all the rest) and jerk the wire that fired the first shot as a signal for the opening of the greatest battle ever fought on the American Continent. I saw the shell when it exploded in the air over the enemy's line, which extended just in front of the skirt of timber as far as we could see both to the right and left. They were in the wheat, however, lying down, though plainly seen, while their officers rode up and down their lines. As soon as the shell from our gun exploded I noticed the smoke rise from one of their guns. Then came the report and shell which exploded over our heads, but did no damage.

In the meantime we had thrown out a skirmish line. J. B. Gambrell, now a noted Baptist divine in Texas, was then a gallant young lieutenant and a member of our regiment, and no braver man ever lived. He was given command of our skirmishers, who soon became engaged all along the line, while the artillery duel began. We moved forward while our line of skirmishers kept pressing back that of the enemy.

After we had advanced through the wheat, across the valley, and up the slope to within good shot of their line, they jumped to their feet and opened fire on us. We continued advancing and firing. They began to fall back until we had reached a shallow railroad cut, where they met with reenforcements. In this cut a hand-to-hand fight took place. Soon they gave way and were driven through the streets of the town. Lieutenant General Reynolds, in command of the Federal forces, was killed in front of our regiment near the railroad.

I was wounded at the railroad cut. A Minie ball struck me on my instep and broke the bones of my foot, lodging against the heel leader. I am thankful that it was not in the heel. The wound was most painful. I was taken back a few yards to where I found four others of my company wounded about the same time that I was. They were Weems, Humphreys, Wilson, and Keeys. Wilson died a few minutes later. Keeys, being shot in the arm, was able to walk and passed on to the rear, leaving Weems, Humphreys, and myself. Our place of "safety" was very much exposed, as shot and shell were tearing up the earth all about us.

Now, I have given an exact statement as to the manner in which the opening of the battle actually occurred. Some historians ignore Heth's Division, which actually opened the battle. In looking over several school histories I find things which I know from personal knowledge are untrue. It seems impossible to get an impartial history of the War of the States. Gen. J. R. Davis's brigade of Mississippians (of Heth's Division), including the 55th North Carolina, to which I belonged, fought every day, while at least two-thirds of the army fought only on the second and third days.

When General Lee saw the cut-up and worn-out condition of our men on the third day in the field, he remarked that they should not be there.

My company entered the battle on the first day with forty-six men. On the night of the third day, after all was over, only two remained for duty. They were Rufus Jones and Berry Scott.

CHAPTER IX

Shortly after being shot and before my wound was dressed I began to cramp. The pain was so severe that I yelled for help. Never have I felt such agony. James Schell, now a citizen of Aberdeen, Miss., who had been an old schoolmate of mine, and a member of the 11th Mississippi Regiment, heard my cry and ran to me, calling for more help. Two others came, and the three rubbed my leg vigorously and drenched me with brandy. As soon as I was relieved somewhat Jim called a surgeon to come and cut for the ball. Jim and the two others got astride of me, holding me to the ground, while the surgeon cut with his knife. It felt like he was using one that he had kept on hand for sharpening slate pencils. After probing he took some tweezers and began searching for the ball, which he soon extricated and handed to me, remarking that I would get a furlough. I have the ball to-day.

Jim dressed my wound nicely; also that of Weems, who was shot through the thigh, and that of Humphreys, who was shot in the right side and liver, a wound that proved fatal. Then an old oilcloth was spread on the ground by some of the field nurses, and we were all three placed on it with a rock each for a pillow, Humphreys being placed in the center. Jim Schell told me that I was going into lockjaw, which was the reason I had cramped so. A man shot in the foot died of lockjaw within a few feet of me just before I began to cramp. The poor fellow did not get the attention I did, as all the surgeons and assistants were busy; so I feel that I am indebted to Jim for my existence at this time, and I am sorry that I have not added more to the credit column of his good deeds account.

Our wounds were redressed once by the surgeon before General Lee began falling back on the fourth day, taking all his wounded that were able to sit upright in ambulances. Weems, Humphreys, and I were not taken. I begged hard to go, and was taken to an ambulance a few feet away, but became so sick that I could not hold up my head. The surgeon then told me that I could not travel, that I would fall into the hands of the enemy, but would be paroled in a few days. All the time that he was saying this to me Weems and Humphreys were begging me to remain with them, so I consented.

On the morning of July 5, about thirty minutes after General Lee's rear guard had passed out of sight, a long line of Union cavalry, mostly dismounted, came along gathering up guns, breaking them and dropping them. A few feet in front of us one of the men picked up a gun, caught it at the muzzle, and, raising the stock end high over his head, intended to break it on a rock in front of him. As it struck the rock it exploded, killing him instantly. I felt like the little boy who dropped and broke his jug containing molasses and, seeing it run over the ground, exclaimed: "O for a thousand tongues!" Only with me it was: "O for a thousand such guns!"

The movements and actions of the enemy fully convinced me that they did not want to interfere any more with General Lee, and were not certain that he had left; they also feared that he might return for the guns. Not a word was spoken to us by any of them; so there we were prisoners of a civil war and expecting to be treated as such, though it turned out very differently. What I say in regard to our treatment has never before been published, except in a short article that I wrote two years ago for my county paper. The treatment so much complained of by prisoners at Andersonville and other places was mild in comparison. No attention whatever had we until Weems and I were taken up on the evening of July 18, Humphreys having died on the 15th. No sooner had breath left his body than two soldiers dragged him by the heels from between us to the front some six or eight feet, where they covered him slightly with shovels of dirt. Such was the manner of burial of another of our noble young men like Crompton at Gaines's Farm.

If the good Lord had not sent us rain every day, we would have perished for water. There happened to be a few small gullies that would hold a canteen or two of water some six or eight spaces from us to which Weems and I would crawl the best we could, fill our canteens, then crawl back to our oilcloth and proceed to dress our wounds, using the same bandages, but washing them each day. I would assist Weems with his wound, he in turn would assist me, and we both together would dress the wound of Humphreys. The water was the same which had fallen on the field where dozens of dead men lay covered, just as they had fallen, with only a few shovels of dirt, also hundreds of dead horses. This we had to drink during our stay of about seventeen days, except the four days before General Lee left the field; and during the time on two occasions when a passing soldier dropped us some hard-tack and a small piece of salt pork the latter had to be eaten uncooked. No doubt hundreds perished for lack of water and attention. I feel satisfied that if either Mr. Lincoln or General Meade had been informed of this needless, cruel neglect he would not have allowed it.

Immediately upon General Lee's departure from the field the Federals began to look after their own wounded and burying their dead. This was to be expected, and was not complained of; but after that, instead of helping us poor suffering and dying Confederates, they engaged in destroying old guns and hauling captured supplies to the railroad. True, they threw a few shovels of dirt over our dead. The horses they dragged up into long rows, attempting to burn them. They failed in this, but raised a fearful stench. Our utterly cruel treatment was caused by some subordinate who no doubt was denied cool drinks and who was not where the weary are at rest. It was there that I discovered in advance of General Sherman that war was h——.

Gen. Stephen D. Lee the year before his death heard of my treatment from some one and sent for me. When we met, he told me what he had heard in regard to our treatment on the battle field of Gettysburg as prisoners of war, and wanted to know if such was the fact. I assured him that it was true just as he had heard it, and that I had a living witness, W. K. Weems, at Baldwin, Miss., who shared the same cruelty with me. He then asked me why they neglected us so long. I answered the same as I have here written. He then said: "Well, well! That surpasses anything that I ever read or heard of in civil warfare."

On July 6 Mr. Lincoln, with several of his Cabinet and a large cavalry escort, rode over the field. They passed just in front of us. Had I known then that Mr. Lincoln was the good man he was and could have gotten an audience with him, I was in a condition to have offered him some overtures that were not considered at the Hampton Roads meeting, which might have been acceptable with him and restored peace whereby thousands of lives would have been saved.

Late in the afternoon of July 18 a Dutchman with his dump cart halted in front of us and ordered Weems and myself to crawl in, "and be d—— quick about it," which we did as soon as we could gather our effects together. My entire wardrobe and furniture consisted of the following articles: One short army shirt, one old sockless and stringless brogan shoe, one flopped hat with a hole in the crown through which my hair of long growth hung out, giving me the appearance of the wild boy from Bitter Creek, and one greasy haversack containing my pocketknife and empty pocketbook; also the pocketbook and gold ring that had belonged to Charley Humphreys. My furniture consisted of one pair of rude crutches that I had made with my pocketknife. My trousers were worn out to the waistband before the battle. I had held on to the waistband, its use being to hold my shirt in position. However, while lying on the field I found it to be a perfect incubator for graybacks, so I discarded it. Weems had the advantage of me in worldly effects in that he did possess a pair of seatless and kneeless trousers. My army jacket had also worn out and felt uncomfortable because of the hot weather, so I let that go with my waistband.

Our Dutchman soon had us jolting over a stony field. As the sun was setting he dumped us out by the side of the railroad track along with about two hundred and fifty other wounded who had been gathered up during the day. Here we all remained overnight. I noticed as we approached the railroad a pile of old broken guns from six to eight feet high extending along the track for several yards.

CHAPTER X

That night a train of cattle arrived which were unloaded the next morning, and those same cars, uncleaned, were backed up to us and we were ordered to get in. This we did with much difficulty and pain. We were soon off, though none of us could learn our destination.

A few months ago United States Senator Col. James Gordon, of Mississippi, was banqueted in Memphis, when some old war papers were read and listened to with much interest. One was a letter from a Federal officer to his superior wherein he made great complaint about the treatment he had received at our hands while a prisoner of war, being conveyed to some place in a cold box car. I was glad to hear of this, for I felt that I had found one Yankee that I could even up with, though I would far rather travel in a refrigerator than in the filthy stock cars we were forced to use.

We soon reached York City, Pa., where the bridge had been wrecked, and we were delayed. While there our car doors were crowded with citizens of all ages and descriptions begging us to take the oath of allegiance to the United States, promising if we complied that we would be provided with a home and would be well cared for until the war was over, when money would be provided to send us home. Of the two hundred and fifty naked, starved, and crippled Confederates, not one accepted the proposition. While there the doubt as to our final success that had begun to form in my mind when Jackson was killed was strengthened. I saw a crowd of young men and older ones subject to military duty dressed in citizen's clothes, and knew that all such in our Confederacy were in service. With the overwhelming majority the Federals had in the field, with such a surplus in the Northern States from which to draw and the ports all open to them, the thought overwhelmed me as to how we could ever hope to overcome such gigantic obstacles.

We were soon moving back over our same route with no knowledge obtainable as to our destination until we reached the city of Baltimore. By some means our lady friends and sympathizers there had learned of our coming, and hundreds were at the station with baskets filled with everything good to eat. As our train stopped and before any of us alighted they rushed for the car doors, falling over each other in their eagerness to be the first to greet us. Basket after basket was pushed in to us, and the way we poor fellows did eat! There was enough left to feed many times our number.

We were then ordered to leave the cars. I had been hoping that the sweet women and girls would retire before I had to get out clad as I was, though there were many in the same fix. Some of the ladies had brought clothing for us, but were not allowed to distribute it. A double line was formed along the cars, and I slipped in, taking my position in the rear rank, using the front rank for a blind and the cars for a background. When in line, we were ordered to left face and move off. Some of us were on crutches; others used sticks, boards, or anything available. On reaching the first street we were ordered to file right in the center. Down the street we went to the wharf on the bay, where we were to embark. The population were jammed thick to watch us; even the housetops were covered. A heavy guard walked on both sides of us as we slowly moved along. I think we were the first prisoners of war that had ever entered the city, and I am sure a more motley crew was never seen. All of us were wounded and represented nearly every Southern State. Many tears of sympathy were shed for us as we marched. I overheard one well-dressed aged lady, who was weeping, remark that she had five boys in the Confederate service and wished she had as many more. For this she was arrested. Several arrests were made as we passed along. No doubt there are many grandmothers in Baltimore to-day who will recall this incident which took place in the afternoon of July 19, 1863.

After reaching the wharf, we had to remain there an hour for preparations to be made on the steamship Nellie Pentze, which was to take us. While waiting I stood leaning on my crutches, my left leg swollen up to my body and greatly inflamed, when a sweet young lady about sixteen years old approached me with her servant, who carried a basket well filled with packages of nice cake. She handed me two of the packages and began to converse with me. She first wanted to know my native State and all about my relatives. She said she was sorry she was not allowed to give me clothing. I was in no spirit, clad as I was, to converse with such a charming creature, although I could not miss the opportunity.

When we went aboard our vessel, I took my position on deck for better or worse, mostly the latter. Not one of us had been solicited to take the oath of allegiance while in the city of Baltimore. We moved off down the bay. It was a lovely sunset evening, and, looking back, we could see thousands of hats and handkerchiefs waving us farewell. We were soon out at sea. During the night a heavy thunderstorm arose. The sails were hauled down and the sailors were running everywhere, seemingly excited. I remained on deck, where the lightning flashed across me every few moments, followed by sprays of water that drenched me. Our ship was tossed like a cracker box. When the storm subsided, we were a very sick set.

CHAPTER XI

July 20 came and still no land was in sight, nor could we determine our destination. During the day there were three deaths from wounds. They received a sea burial. Early on the 22d we spied land, much to our relief. Soon we entered the bay at New York, thence up East River to the north end of Long Island, where there was a long, narrow island eighty acres in area called David's Island. Here the Federals had elected twenty-two pavilions in a line, with a mess room between each two. The building extended nearly the entire length of the island. Each pavilion was divided into four wards which contained twenty cots each. A doctor's office stood in front and a bathroom in the rear. This pavilion had been used by their soldiers as a hospital, and had just been vacated. As there were 2,500 Confederates on the island, tents had to be erected in order to accommodate all.

Upon our arrival we were at once divested of all wearing apparel, which was burned, and each one given a bath. Then a hospital suit was provided, which consisted of a long gray gown fastened at the waist with a green cord, also hose and blue cloth slippers. I was consigned to Pavilion 4, Ward 1. Irish women were employed to scrub the floors daily, and everything was kept neat. There was a large steam laundry kept going constantly for the use of all. In one large general kitchen food was prepared and sent to mess rooms, and there were several "lady" kitchens where fancy dishes were prepared for the sickest patients. The diet was changed each day, and it was good. Those not able to go to the mess room were served at their cots. There was only one church, Episcopal, which we attended when able. We had access to a good library; in fact, the whole island was at our disposal. When the tide went out, we gathered clams for bait and fished. We had moved from Hades to heaven, and everything possible was done for our comfort. Everybody was pleasant to us; my own nurse was like a brother. I hated being a prisoner, though, and detested the arrangement of flowers in spelling the words "Constitution," "Union," and "Abraham Lincoln."

Many sympathizers from New York visited us every day and brought things. A number of deaths occurred, caused by gangrene. When as many as two hundred and fifty or three hundred were able to travel, they were given a suit of clothing and sent away to be paroled. I had gangrene and was in the last squadron moved. The clothing given was from our friends in the city. The suits for the last squadron were a little nicer than any previously given. I was very proud of mine. The coat was a seal-brown frock with a double row of staff buttons in front.

There was a very long gangway extending from the ground to the deck of the vessel along which we had to pass in single file. At the foot of this six or eight soldiers were standing. As I approached one of them ordered me to take off my coat. This I reluctantly did, some one holding my crutches for me. The soldier took it and cut off every button, then handed it to two other soldiers, who twisted it as tight as they could and held it over a block, while another with an ax whacked off the tail just below the waist. They then handed the body part back to me, which I refused to accept, tossing it into the water. I was mad. All of us were treated in the same manner. Some sensibly put the remainder of their coats on, as the weather was cold. This was the only mean act toward us while there, and none of those who had gone before us received such treatment.

While sailing down the bay at New York we passed many gunboats anchored at different places doing picket duty. As we passed the captain was hailed by the commander of each boat and asked our destination. He, a perfect giant in statue, was standing on deck where I lay with the toes of his No. 14 shoes jammed in my side. He answered: "Fortress Monroe." "What is your cargo?" was then asked. In a voice like a fog horn the captain answered: "D— bobtail Rebels." I wished I was a David with a good sling shot so I could have presented his head to Mr. Davis.

On our arrival at Fortress Monroe we were transferred to a steamboat that carried us up the James River to City Point, below Richmond, where we were to be paroled. Our boat landed, all of us eager enough to again stand in dear old Dixie. We were not allowed to go ashore for about an hour, when the oath was administered to each one and we were free. The first question I asked was if Vicksburg and Port Hudson were still holding out. Both places had surrendered, so the Northern papers stated, the day I was captured.

A train was in readiness that carried us to Petersburg. On arriving there we were consigned to our different State hospitals. I was placed in the South Carolina hospital, as Mississippi did not have one. Here I found a vast difference in the food compared to that of David's Island. It was the best our poor country could furnish. The tea and coffee were fearful; the tea tasted like tobacco stems. I remained here a few days awaiting the meeting of the medical board, who were to examine wounds and grant furloughs. I was granted sixty days. I then requested transportation, and was soon on my way home.

CHAPTER XII

The railroads were badly damaged, so it took a long time to reach a place a short distance away. I noticed that a great change had taken place during my confinement of four months. Everything seemed so desolate. When I reached Okolona, Miss., I learned that the enemy had visited our section, taking everything. My own family, having been left without substance, had been taken to a place of hiding by some faithful old darkies. I secured a horse and an old darky to pilot me, and started for that section of the country where I had been told they had gone. The following day I met one of our servants, who was overjoyed to see me and told me that mother was about two miles away. We turned into an old blind road with bushes in the center and followed it a mile, reaching a scrub pine field. In the center of this field stood a double log cabin, the refuge of my family. Notwithstanding the surroundings, our meeting was a happy one. I found that the Yankees had taken from my mother everything, and those faithful darkies had done odd jobs to get meat and bread for the family.

After a few days at home, my wound inflamed and I was confined to my bed for some time. Before my sixty days' furlough was out the medical board of the county extended it sixty days longer. Before the expiration of that time a cavalry company was organized, which I joined, thinking I would no longer be useful for infantry service. I was elected first lieutenant by a handsome majority and secured the goods for a uniform, having a tailor make it who charged the most outrageous price. An uncle furnished me a good horse, and I was soon equipped and ready.

Our company was an independent one, the government furnishing nothing. After all was in readiness, we moved off to locate the enemy. As soon as we located them, finding that they were too numerous, we turned our attention to locating smaller forces. We were brave all right, but no company in the army could surpass us in prudence. Occasionally we would not locate the enemy in time, and would be forced to exchange a few shots, but not many. Dave Braden told this joke on our company: He had been wounded and was unable to serve in the infantry, his wound crippling him for life. He could have been discharged, but such was not his wish. Well, Dave started out to find our company, intending to join us. He wore a Yankee overcoat. He heard that we were at Iuka, Miss., and made for that place. On reaching there he was told that we had only a few hours before passed through Iuka going southward. He said he moved on with as little delay as possible, hoping to overtake us. Often he would see a cavalryman in full tilt disappear at the turn of the road; but he thought nothing of this, as the common practice with cavalrymen was to be running. One warm day some distance south of Selma, Ala., he pulled off his Yankee overcoat and sat upon it. He then overtook the fleeing cavalryman, who said he was our rear guard and that the enemy had been pursuing him all the way from Iuka, Miss.

We decided to attach ourselves to some regiment, which was soon accomplished. This was a foolish act on our part, for in a few days we were dismounted and sent as infantry by rail to take part in the battle of Harrisburg, Miss. After this battle we were ordered direct by rail to Atlanta, Ga., and there placed in the ditches, where we took part in the battle on July 28, after which we went to Selma, Ala., where our horses had been sent. They were in a bad condition.

At this time I was appointed to detail certain disabled men and some unserviceable horses, appointing well men to look after them, and to select some suitable place for a recruiting camp. This easy appointment came through a friendship existing between my father and his colonel.

After gathering my command together with a few wagons and tents, I proceeded with my caravan to a chain of mountains in Alabama, where I found an ideal spot and a large spring of cold water. In the valley was excellent grazing for the horses. Here I proceeded to appoint my commissioned and noncommissioned officers—captains and lieutenants, also quartermaster and commissary—with full power to act as if appointed by the head of the government.

To give an idea of war prices in the South I mention that a pair of cotton cards formerly priced at fifty cents sold then for $80. Salt was $80 per sack and butter $4 per pound; while a night's lodging was about $15.

My temporary surgeon called at my quarters and said that his sick men needed stimulants. All government distilleries had shut down for want of material, and whisky was issued only to those fatally wounded on the field and to favorite officers who would not be denied. I hadn't enough money to purchase the article which had to be bought from moonshiners. We had several soreback government horses, the only kind on the market, as all horses in good condition were pressed into service. I had no trouble in selling one which was pronounced incurable for $1,500.

After being sworn to secrecy, I was piloted to the locality of the still whose owner was an Irishman. The still consisted of two large washpots, the top one upside down. A narrow wooden arm about four feet long and five inches in diameter extended from the pots to a small dogwood sapling around which two or three gun barrels had been twisted and the end attached to the arm and used as a worm. This, with a few hollow gum tubes, composed the outfit. They had on hand one barrel of stimulants said to contain thirty-seven and a half gallons at $40 per gallon, F. O. B. the slide, the only mode of conveyance, as there was no wagon road. The amount came to exactly $1,500, the price paid for the horse. On its arrival in camp there was no delay in opening it. Our chemist pronounced it one-fourth meal, one-fourth sorghum cane seed, one-fourth china berries, and one-fourth pine tops. Our doctor said it would do, as no other was to be found, and instructed his sick to use it freely, internally, externally, and eternally, and he did likewise. In a few days he cited me to the rosy cheeks of his patients, which I had already noticed. About the time the barrel was empty I received orders to report to our command with our men and horses. On our arrival there our comrades wanted to know why there were so many red eyes and noses. We answered: "Mountain air."

Our captain was wounded and permanently disabled on July 28, 1864, at Atlanta, Ga., though he would never resign, which disappointed me, as I was first lieutenant and wanted to be captain by promotion. During my absence the company had been in command of our second lieutenant and were in camp about eight miles from Rome, Ga., which was occupied by the enemy. It was growing late in the fall of '64, and the enemy had such a stronghold in Georgia, Alabama, and Mississippi, with all supplies cut off, that all we could do was to keep out of the way.

A few days after our return to our command I concluded to hunt something to eat better than we had in camp. I took the main road that led to Rome. After going a few miles, I found a place where I was told I could obtain something. The good lady of the house at once prepared my dinner, which consisted of a cup of good corn meal coffee, corn dodgers, baked sweet potatoes, sorghum molasses, and buttermilk. I enjoyed the feast very much. After paying for same, I was returning to camp when I heard a voice to my right at the top of a hill calling "Halt!" I looked and saw five or six mounted bluecoats. My horse and I took in the situation at once. I got flat on his back, pressed both spurs into his side, and flew. "Halt! halt! halt!" Bang! bang! zip! zip! came the bullets. We were going at such a gait that we could not halt. The fence rails seemed a sheet of solid timber. The Yankees kept shooting until the road turned into timber. They must have been poor shots or did not want to hurt us, for not a scratch was made upon me or upon my horse except that a ball had passed through one end of my blanket, which was rolled and strapped to the back of my saddle. Often a man would be sent out as a decoy, leading those in pursuit to be fired upon from ambush. Probably they mistook me for a decoy.

Several days later I decided to ride out again in a different direction, accompanied by Lieutenant Foster, of our regiment. We went about three miles and found a place where a similar dinner was served us as previously described. On our return we heard a voice in our rear calling on us to halt, and found that eight or ten Yankee cavalrymen were in full tilt after us. We had several hundred yards the start and moved at breakneck speed. A small creek had to be forded, the water being about two feet deep, which we crossed in a gallop. As we reached the opposite bank, Foster's horse stumbled and fell to his knees, Foster going over his head, pulling off the horse's bridle as he passed over. He started on foot as fast as he could, yelling to me to wait. I replied that I would do so at the judge's stand. His horse got on his feet and galloped after Foster, soon overtaking him. How far the Yankees followed us we could not tell. I decided after this experience to live on such food as we had in camp.

I could not understand why we were kept at one place so long. We were too weak to stop the advance of a small army and there was nothing to protect, as the country had been divested of everything, both armies having occupied it. We would go out occasionally, have a little skirmish, and have a man or two killed. The Creator never made men equal to the Confederate soldier. For many months none of us had the least hope of success, yet we would stand and be shot at for our country. Our poor government had about exhausted supplies of every kind and had not paid any of her soldiers for months. For example, my own claim (unpaid at the surrender) as first lieutenant in cavalry at $90 per month for fourteen months amounted to $1,260. Notwithstanding all rations were cut short, complaints were seldom heard.

Winter was fast approaching when we were ordered into Alabama and from there to Mississippi, where we were constantly on the move. The enemy was everywhere and we had little territory in which to operate. We were at no time longer than two or three days at one place, having to hunt food for man and beast. Occasionally a remote neighborhood could be found that had not been molested, but not often.

The first month of the spring of '65 found us pitifully subsisting upon anything obtainable. We were near Selma, Ala., when the news came of General Lee's surrender. It was no surprise to us.

Thus ended the severest war ever fought in this country or any other. Father against son, brother against brother! My father had an only brother who was a surgeon of an Illinois regiment in the Union army; while my father, Maj. E. L. Hankins, served throughout the war in the Confederate army, commanding Ashcraft's Regiment, composed of the 2d and 3d Battalions of Mississippi Cavalry. There were hundreds of similar cases.

The time is growing near when there will be none of us left to tell the "story of the glory of the men who wore the gray," so I have made the foregoing contribution of my experiences in this "Simple Story of a Soldier."

INDEX